BLAST BACK!

THE STATUE OF LIBERTY

by Nancy Ohlin   illustrated by Roger Simó

D0204301

little bee books

CONTENTS

Introduction

You've probably heard of the Statue of Liberty and seen it in pictures or even in person. But have you ever wondered why it was built—and when, and how? What does the statue have to do with liberty, anyway? Let's blast back in time for a little adventure and find out. . . .

A Brief History of the Statue of Liberty

The Statue of Liberty is a statue of Libertas, the Roman goddess of liberty, wearing a crown. She holds a torch in her right hand. In her left hand is a tablet inscribed with the date July 4, 1776, when the Declaration of Independence was adopted, in Roman numerals.

The statue is located in New York City. It sits on Liberty Island, formerly called Bedloe's Island, in Upper New York Bay (aka New York Harbor), just off the southern tip of Manhattan Island (a part of New York City). It is 305 feet tall including its pedestal (and 151 feet without the pedestal) and weighs 450,000 pounds. The torch on its own measures twenty-nine feet from top to bottom.

To date, it is one of the largest statues ever built.

The idea for the Statue of Liberty was conceived by a small group of Frenchmen in 1865. It was meant to honor the friendship between the U.S. and France, the end of slavery in the U.S., and the principals of democracy. (Democracy is a form of government in which all citizens are able to participate, either directly or through elected representatives or both.)

However, its eventual construction became a joint venture and not an outright gift from the French. Americans had to raise a lot of money to help complete the project. The finished statue was unveiled in 1886. Its formal name is Liberty Enlightening the World, which is a translation of the French name, *La Liberté éclairant le monde*. It is sometimes referred to as "Lady Liberty."

A symbol of freedom and democracy, the Statue of Liberty has welcomed millions of immigrants to the U.S.

The U.S. in the Mid- to Late 1800s

The mid- to late 1800s was a time of great change for the United States. The American Civil War took place between the Union (which consisted mostly of the northern states) and the Confederacy (which consisted mostly of the southern states), in part over the issue of slavery. The war began in 1861 and ended in 1865. After the war, the law was changed to end slavery and allow freedmen (former slaves) to become U.S. citizens.

The mid- to late 1800s also saw the rise of industrialization, and many factories were built to manufacture goods on a mass scale. Important industries included steel, which was used for (among other things) building railroads, and petroleum, which was used for (among other things) heating and lighting.

In 1882, Thomas Edison introduced an electric lighting system to New York City, which launched the age of electricity. Other inventions around this time include the typewriter, telephone, and automobile.

The U.S. population grew tremendously in the nineteenth century as immigrants from other countries arrived to seek better lives for themselves and their families. The 1880s especially saw a massive increase in immigrants. This, along with prejudice against foreigners and other factors, led to laws restricting the number of immigrants who could enter the U.S.

CHINESE EXCLUSION ACT
1882
es of America
Congre
IMMIGRATION ACT OF 1882
Congress of U
erica
ALIEN CONTRACT LABOR
LAWS OF 1885
OF STATES OF AMERICA
ALIEN CONTRACT LABOR
LAWS OF 1885
CONGRESS OF THE UNITED STATES OF AMERICA

Anti-Immigration Laws

In 1875, the U.S. Supreme Court declared that the federal government, not the states, should be in charge of immigration. The U.S. Congress proceeded to enact a number of anti-immigration laws. For example, the Chinese Exclusion Act of 1882 prohibited the immigration of all Chinese laborers. (It also limited the ability of Chinese nonlaborers to immigrate to the U.S.) It was the first American immigration law to target a specific ethnic group, and it was not repealed, or reversed, until 1943. Other anti-immigration laws included the Immigration Act of 1882 and the Alien Contract Labor Laws of 1885 and 1887.

Ellis Island

In 1890, Congress set aside $75,000 to build the country's first federally operated immigration center. In 1892, the center opened on Ellis Island in New York Harbor. On the first day, 700 immigrants were processed at Ellis Island. In the first year, the number reached close to 450,000. By the time the center closed in 1954, an estimated 12 million immigrants had been processed through Ellis Island.

Ellis Island is a quick ferry ride from Liberty Island, where the Statue of Liberty stands.

France in the Mid- to Late 1800s

From the 1850s to the 1870s, France was led by an emperor named Charles-Louis-Napoléon Bonaparte, or Napoleon III. (He was the nephew of the famous emperor Napoleon I.) Napoleon III believed in an authoritarian form of government and in limiting the rights of French citizens.

In 1870, France went to war against Prussia, which controlled the German states. (There was no unified Germany until 1871.) This war was called the Franco-Prussian War and lasted from 1870 to 1871. France was badly defeated, and the reign of Napoleon III came to an end. A new system of government, called the Third Republic, was established in France in 1875 and consisted of a president, a cabinet, and a parliament. The Third Republic lasted for sixty-five years and was full of instability and conflict, with many different political parties fighting for power.

Despite all this, France experienced economic and cultural advancements during this time. It produced some of the greatest writers in history (including Victor Hugo, Gustave Flaubert, Alexandre Dumas, Jules Verne, and Marcel Proust) as well as some of the greatest artists (including Henri Matisse, Edouard Manet, Claude Monet, Berthe Morisot, Edgar Degas, and Pierre-Auguste Renoir).

The Beginnings of the Statue of Liberty

The idea for the Statue of Liberty came to life at a dinner party in 1865. The dinner party took place at the home of Édouard de Laboulaye just outside of Paris, France. Laboulaye was a historian, law professor, politician, and the head of the French Anti-Slavery Society. He and his guests were great believers in democracy. They were considered to be radicals in their time because they opposed the authoritarian rule of Napoleon III.

Laboulaye felt that the United States was a shining example of democracy and wanted to honor and celebrate its values. He proposed they build some sort of monument as a gift to the U.S. that could be built in France and presented to the Americans in 1876, on the hundredth anniversary of their independence from the British.

In 1870, French sculptor Frédéric-Auguste Bartholdi—who had been one of the guests at that dinner party—began sketches for a possible design for the monument. In 1871 and 1872, Bartholdi traveled around the U.S. to talk about the monument with Americans and try to get them excited about it.

On this trip, Bartholdi visited Bedloe's Island in New York Harbor and decided that it would be a perfect home for the monument. There, it would be visible to all ships arriving in New York, which he thought of as a "gateway to America."

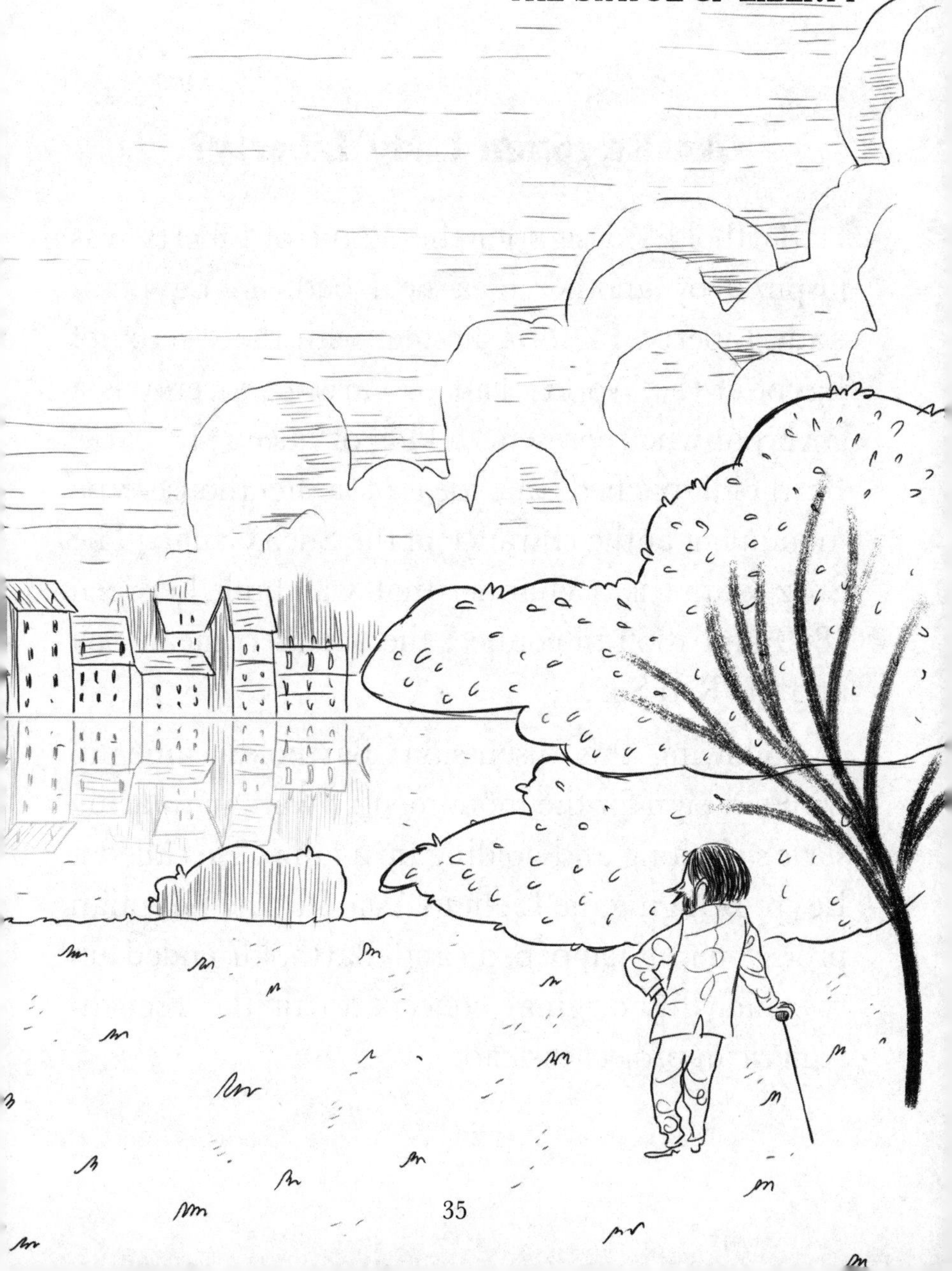

An Egyptian Lady Liberty?

Bartholdi's design for the Statue of Liberty was inspired by another idea he'd had: an Egyptian Lady Liberty. In 1867, he met with the viceroy of Egypt at the World's Fair in Paris. (A viceroy is a governor who represents a king or queen.) In Paris, Bartholdi pitched the idea of a lighthouse-type monument at the entrance of the Suez Canal. (The Suez Canal is a channel that was built between 1859 and 1869 to connect the Mediterranean Sea and the Red Sea.)

Following this discussion, Bartholdi came up with a design for the monument: a woman wearing slave's clothing and holding up a lamp. He called it Egypt Bringing the Light to Asia. But the Egyptian project never happened, and Bartholdi ended up tweaking his original concept to fit the French-American project instead.

The Franco-American Union

Between 1874 and 1875, a committee was formed in France with Laboulaye as its president. The committee's purpose was to oversee plans for the monument and raise funds to build it.

The members decided that the actual building of the monument should be a joint French-American venture, with the French constructing the statue and transporting it to the U.S., and the Americans providing its site and building the pedestal (or base). Several committees were formed in the U.S. to be counterparts to the French committee. The French and American committees together were called the Franco-American Union.

In 1875, the French committee approved Bartholdi's design for the statue, and fund-raising for the actual building of the monument began. Laboulaye also made a formal request to President Ulysses S. Grant (via the U.S. ambassador to France, Levi P. Morton) to have Bedloe's Island be the home for the finished monument.

Raising Money

The members of the French committee raised money for the monument in a number of ways, including lotteries, fetes (or parties), and the selling of souvenirs (such as miniature versions of the monument). Bartholdi even charged money to allow people to watch the statue being constructed in his Paris workshop.

Renowned composer Charles Gounod also pitched in to help the cause. He wrote a ten-minute choral piece called "Liberty Enlightening the World" and conducted its premiere performance at the Paris Opera in April of 1876.

The American committees had a harder time with fund-raising. The American public was not very enthusiastic about the monument project. For one thing, they weren't sure if the project would ever be completed. They didn't have much confidence that the French would be able to raise the necessary funds. Also, many Americans weren't crazy about the proposed Bedloe's Island site for the monument. They felt this location would make the monument a New York City monument and not a national monument. Some made fun of the monument by calling it "New York's lighthouse."

Gradual Progress

By 1876, the French had raised enough money to at least get started on the monument. That year, Bartholdi began building the statue in France. He finished the torch and hand, which were shipped to the U.S. for display. (By this point, the French had missed their deadline of giving the monument to the Americans by 1876, the centennial year of their independence from the British.)

In 1877, President Grant signed a bill approving the use of Bedloe's Island for the monument. Construction continued in France, and in 1878, the head and shoulders were completed and displayed at the Paris Universal Exposition.

In 1879, the engineer on the project, Eugène-Emmanuel Viollet-le-Duc, died and was replaced by Alexandre-Gustave Eiffel. In 1880, Eiffel completed the inner framework for the statue, which was made of wood and four huge steel supports. The framework was then covered with copper sheets that had been hammered into shape by hand.

Alexandre-Gustave Eiffel

Eiffel was a French engineer who specialized in bridges and other metal structures. In 1886, he won a competition to design a monument for the 1889 World's Fair in Paris. His design was built in a record two years and considered to be a technological marvel, earning him the nickname "Magician of Iron." Today, the Eiffel Tower is one of the most famous and iconic structures in the world.

The Lighthouse of Liberty?

When President Grant approved the use of Bedloe's Island for the monument, he added the condition that it be a lighthouse. That way, it would serve a useful purpose, and he could justify spending government money on the project.

But it turned out that the engineers were not able to "light up" the monument enough to make it work as a lighthouse. Bedloe's Island also proved to be too far inland to be a good lighthouse location.

Bedloe's Island

Bedloe's Island had a long and interesting history before becoming the home of the Statue of Liberty.

Around 994, Native Americans came to the island and settled there. The island was known as one of the three "Oyster Islands" in New York Harbor because of the plentiful oysters.

But in 1609, the British explorer Henry Hudson arrived in New York Harbor, and soon after, Europeans began to colonize the Oyster Islands and the surrounding area. The original Native American inhabitants were forced to leave and try to find new homes to the north and west.

For the next two centuries, Bedloe's Island had many different owners and uses. It was a Dutch island, a British island, a Dutch island again, a quarantine station (where passengers on incoming ships were inspected for diseases), a private summer home, the site of a hospital, and a refuge for American colonists who sided with the British during the Revolutionary War.

After the war, Bedloe's Island became a military post to protect New York Harbor. A fort was constructed there between 1809 and 1811. It was built in an eleven-pointed star shape and had mounts for artillery. It was named Fort Wood.

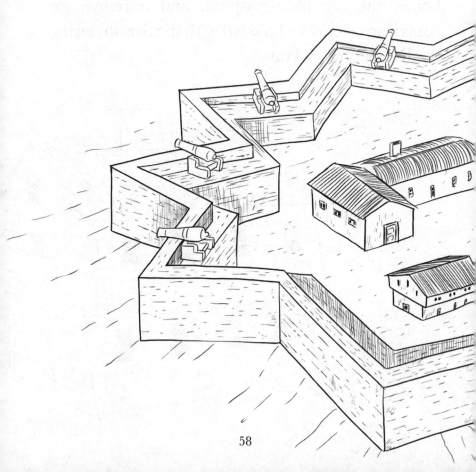

The Fort Wood garrison was disbanded in 1877 (although the U.S. Army continued to maintain a post there until 1937), and Bedloe's Island was designated as the site for the Statue of Liberty. In 1956, Congress officially renamed it Liberty Island.

Other Sites That Were Considered

Other New York sites were considered for the statue, including Central Park in Manhattan and Prospect Park in Brooklyn.

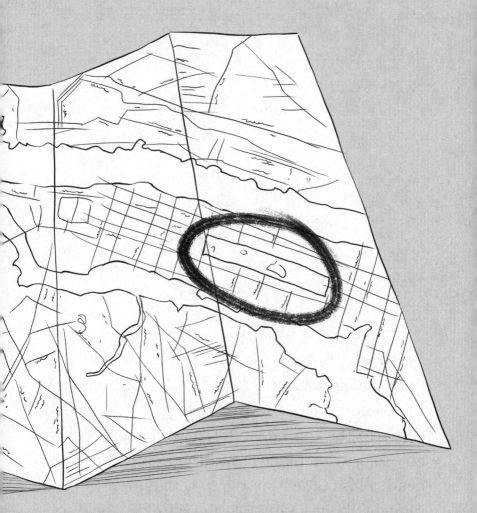

Philadelphia was also considered. In 1876, Bartholdi shipped the finished hand and torch to Philadelphia to be displayed at the Centennial Exposition there. Many people paid admission to climb to the top of the torch, and Bartholdi was able to use that money toward building the statue's head. This made him so happy that for a while, he thought about giving the statue to Philadelphia.

At one point, Boston offered to pay money to become the home for the statue. In response, the *New York Times* printed these words in an editorial: "no third-rate town is going to step in and take it from us."

The Pedestal

In 1882, the Americans learned that the French had raised all the money necessary to complete their part of the project, and that the statue would likely be finished in 1883.

So, in 1883, work began on the pedestal on Bedloe's Island. The designer was Richard Morris Hunt, and the project supervisor was Charles Pomeroy Stone.

The pedestal was sited inside the star-shaped walls of Fort Wood. Building materials included concrete, iron, and stone. The foundation, which was practically solid concrete, was placed twenty feet belowground for stability.

But unfortunately, workers had to stop construction in the fall of 1884, even though they had only completed fifteen feet of the aboveground portion of the pedestal.

Money had run out.

The Final Stretch

In 1884, the French completed work on the statue. On July 4, they handed over official ownership of the statue to the U.S. during a ceremony in Paris.

But the Americans could not resume work on the pedestal due to a lack of funds. The law-making branch of the New York state government had approved $50,000 toward the completion of the pedestal. But Governor Grover Cleveland (who was elected president later that year) vetoed it, saying that it was an unconstitutional use of the people's money.

In 1885, the statue was disassembled in Paris and crated, awaiting shipment to the U.S. Would the Americans be able to raise enough money to finish their part of the project? Or would they have to reject France's gift?

A newspaper publisher named Joseph Pulitzer came to the rescue.

For years, the American newspapers had been very negative about the project, which had not helped the public's attitude toward it. But Pulitzer supported the monument. So he decided to print the name of every person who donated money to the cause, even if it was only a penny.

This turned out to be a wildly successful fund-raising strategy. He managed to raise $50,000 in just two months, and work resumed on the pedestal. By the end of the six-month fund-raising campaign, he had raised more than $100,000.

Joseph Pulitzer

Born in 1847, Joseph Pulitzer emigrated to the U.S. from Hungary in 1864. He fought in the American Civil War for the Union. After the war, he worked as a reporter, then eventually began buying newspaper companies, including the *St. Louis Dispatch*, the *St. Louis Post*, and the *New York World*. He was famous for using catchy headlines, contests, and sensationalism (or exaggerating the truth) to increase readership of his newspapers. He was also a fierce opponent of government corruption. When he died in 1911, he left money to Columbia University in New York City to start a journalism school. He also left money to fund an annual prize for excellence in journalism, drama, and other fields; today, we know this prize as the Pulitzer Prize.

The Statue Arrives in America

In the spring of 1885, the statue portion of the Statue of Liberty crossed the Atlantic in 214 crates on a steam-and-sail gunboat called *Isère*. The person in charge of the shipment was a nineteen-year-old lieutenant named Rodolphe Victor de Drambour.

The ship almost sank in a violent seventy-two-hour storm but managed to survive. On June 17, the *Isère* and her valuable cargo arrived safely in New York Harbor and were greeted by many well-wishers including the *New York World*, the New York Yacht Club, and the U.S. Fleet.

It would be another year before the pedestal was completed and the statue was reassembled on top of the pedestal.

The Changing Colors of Lady Liberty

We think of the Statue of Liberty as being green. But its exterior is made of copper, so its original color was the shiny brown of a new penny. Over several decades, the copper oxidized (combined with oxygen) and developed a patina, or covering, of green over the copper. That green is the color we associate with the statue today.

Monster Disc

In 1877, Thomas Edison invented the phonograph, a device that could record and play back sound on discs (also called "records"). In 1878, he told newspapers that he was going to design a "monster disc" that could be placed inside the statue and allow her to "talk" and "give speeches." The idea was eventually abandoned.

The Unveiling Ceremony

The completed Statue of Liberty was unveiled at a ceremony on October 28, 1886. President Grover Cleveland presided over the event and accepted the gift from the French, saying, "We will not forget that liberty here made her home; nor shall her chosen altar be neglected." Bartholdi dramatically revealed the statue to the crowd—the public had not seen the completed structure until that moment—by unfurling a huge French flag that covered it.

Laboulaye was not at the ceremony; he had passed away in 1883.

Women's rights groups showed up at the ceremony to protest the unveiling of a female statue that supposedly represented liberty when American women had no "liberty" to vote. (American women did not gain the right to vote until 1920, with the Nineteenth Amendment to the Constitution.) Only two women were officially allowed to attend the ceremony: Bartholdi's wife and the teenaged daughter of the French engineer who had designed the Suez Canal.

None of the speeches at the unveiling mentioned immigrants, except for the descendants of French noblemen who had fought with the American colonists against Britain during the Revolutionary War. It was not until much later that people would come to think of the Statue of Liberty as a figure welcoming newcomers to the U.S.

The Crown and the Chain

The seven spikes in the crown represent Lady Liberty's light shining on the seven continents and the seven seas. The broken chain at its feet represents freedom from the shackles of tyranny.

"Give Me Your Tired, Your Poor"

Inscribed on a bronze plaque inside the pedestal's base is a poem called "The New Colossus." Its author was Emma Lazarus.

Born in 1849 in New York City, Lazarus was a poet, essayist, and activist for the rights of immigrants. She wrote essays about anti-Semitism and other types of prejudice. In the 1880s, she became a passionate advocate for Jewish refugees who had fled from Russia to avoid being killed by the government and its followers.

In 1883, she was asked to write a poem that would be sold at an auction along with the works of other authors (such as Walt Whitman and Mark Twain). The purpose of the auction was to raise money for the pedestal. She agreed and wrote "The New Colossus." (The word "colossus" means a giant statue, or something or someone of great size, power, or importance.)

Neither Lazarus nor her poem was mentioned during the unveiling ceremony in 1886, however, and she died a year later at the age of thirty-eight. The poem was rediscovered years later, and in 1903, it was inscribed to a plaque and affixed to the statue. Over a century later, Lazarus's powerful and compassionate words continue to welcome immigrants to American shores.

"The New Colossus" by Emma Lazarus

Not like the brazen giant of Greek fame,

With conquering limbs astride from land to land;

Here at our sea-washed, sunset gates shall stand

A mighty woman with a torch, whose flame

Is the imprisoned lightning, and her name

Mother of Exiles. From her beacon-hand

Glows world-wide welcome; her mild eyes command

The air-bridged harbor that twin cities frame.

"Keep, ancient lands, your storied pomp!" cries she

With silent lips. "Give me your tired, your poor,

Your huddled masses yearning to breathe free,

The wretched refuse of your teeming shore.

Send these, the homeless, tempest-tost to me,

I lift my lamp beside the golden door!"

Lady Liberty, Jr.

In July of 1889, the centennial of an important turning point in the French Revolution, the United States presented France with a miniature version of the Statue of Liberty. At around thirty-seven feet tall, it stands on an island in the Seine River in Paris.

The First 125 Years

Even though the Statue of Liberty wasn't technically a lighthouse, its lit-up torch could provide some aid to ships and boats. So, years after it was unveiled, a governmental agency called the United States Lighthouse Board (which is now part of the U.S. Coast Guard) was put in charge of it.

In 1901, responsibility for the statue was transferred to the U.S. Department of War, since Fort Wood was still an army post. The statue was declared a national monument in 1924, and in 1933, the National Park Service was put in charge of it.

When Fort Wood was deactivated as a military post in 1937, the whole island became part of the national monument, and in 1965, nearby Ellis Island became part of the national monument, too; this increased its total size to about fifty-eight acres.

In 1982, the U.S. government launched a major renovation of the Statue of Liberty in anticipation of the monument's centennial in 1986. American and French architects, engineers, and other workers came together to complete the four-year renovation.

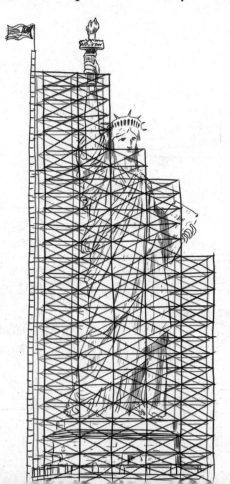

In 1984, the Statue of Liberty was designated as a UNESCO World Heritage site. In 1986, after the completion of the renovations, there was a four-day celebration in honor of the centennial.

In 2001, Liberty Island was closed to the public after the September 11 attacks on the World Trade Center and the Pentagon. It opened again on December 1, although the inside of the monument remained closed. On August 3, 2004, the inside of the pedestal was reopened; on July 4, 2009, the crown was reopened as well.

On October 28, 2011, there was a celebration to honor the 125th anniversary of the statue.

Gifts from Other Countries

Other countries have given gifts to the United States over the years. Here are some famous examples:

• In 1880, Queen Victoria of England gave the Resolute desk to U.S. President Rutherford B. Hayes. It was built from wood from HMS *Resolute*, a British Arctic exploration ship. It sits in the Oval Office of the White House and has been used by many presidents.

• In 1912, Japan gave 3,020 cherry blossom trees to be planted in Washington, D.C.

• China gave two giant pandas, Ling-Ling and Hsing-Hsing, following President Richard Nixon's visit there in 1972.

• In 2006, Russia gave the U.S. a ten-story monument called To the Struggle Against World Terrorism. It stands in Bayonne, New Jersey.

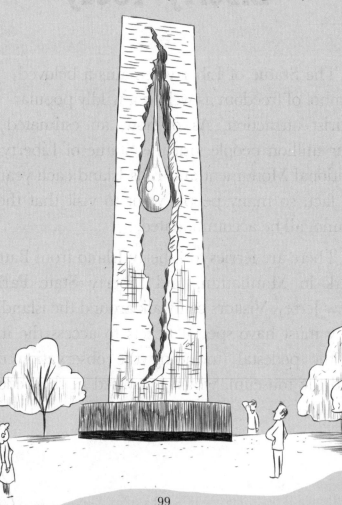

The Statue of Liberty Today

The Statue of Liberty remains a beloved symbol of freedom as well as a wildly popular tourist attraction. As of now, an estimated four million people visit the Statue of Liberty National Monument and Ellis Island each year. In fact, so many people want to visit that they cannot all be accommodated.

There are ferries to Liberty Island from Battery Park in Manhattan, and Liberty State Park in New Jersey. Visitors can walk around the island, but they must have special tickets to access the inside of the pedestal (including the observation deck) and the museum, which is housed in the pedestal.

The observation deck can be reached by elevator or stairway. A small number of visitors each day are also permitted to climb the 354 steps up to the crown via a spiral staircase. (The torch has been off-limits since 1916.)

Construction on a new, larger Statue of Liberty museum began in October of 2016 and will be completed in 2019.

The Statue of Liberty is an iconic image that has been featured in many paintings and drawings and also commemorated on stamps, coins, medals, and other items.

The Legacy of the Statue of Liberty

The Statue of Liberty was built to honor the ideals of democracy. Today, immigrants still come to America's shores to find better lives for themselves and their families. Just as there was prejudice against immigrants when the statue was first unveiled, there is prejudice against immigrants today. The American government continues to try to write and rewrite laws to figure out which people from what countries should be able to enter and stay in the U.S.

In the meantime, Lady Liberty stands solidly on her island perch in New York Bay, the "Mother of Exiles" welcoming the tired and the poor, the homeless and the huddled masses.

Well, it's been a great adventure. Goodbye, Statue of Liberty!

Where to next?

Selected Bibliography

Bartholdi, Frédéric Auguste. *The Statue of Liberty Enlightening the World*.
New York: North American Review, 1885. https://archive.org/details/statuelibertyen00bartgoog.

Britannica Kids. kids.britannica.com.

"Early American Immigration Policies." *US Citizenship and Immigration Services*. September 4, 2015.
https://www.uscis.gov/history-and-genealogy/our-history/agency-history/early-american-immigration-policies.

"Édouard de Laboulaye." *National Park Service*. August 10, 2017.
https://www.nps.gov/stli/learn/historyculture/edouard-de-laboulaye.htm.

Encyclopedia Britannica. www.britannica.com.

Fischer, David Hackett. *Liberty and Freedom: A Visual History of America's Founding Ideas*.
New York: Oxford University Press, 2004.

Mettler, Katie. "'Give Me Your Tired, Your Poor': The Story of Poet and Refugee Advocate Emma Lazarus."
Washington Post. February 1, 2017.
https://www.washingtonpost.com/news/morning-mix/wp/2017/02/01/give-us-your-tired-your-poor-the-story-of-poet-and-refugee-advocate-emma-lazarus/?utm_term=.4c5aae076071.

Mitchell, Elizabeth. *Liberty's Torch: The Great Adventure to Build the Statue of Liberty*.
New York: Atlantic Monthly Press, 2014.

Robertson, Nan. "US Premiere of Hymn to Statue of Liberty." *New York Times*.
February 28, 1985. http://www.nytimes.com/1985/02/28/arts/us-premiere-for-hymn-to-statue-of-liberty.html.

Rothman, Lily. "See Early Photos of the Statue of Liberty Before It Came to New York."
Time. June 17, 2015. http://time.com/3910750/statue-liberty-pictures.

Statue of Liberty–Ellis Island Foundation. http://libertyellisfoundation.org.

"Statue of Liberty." *National Park Service*. September 25, 2000.
https://www.nps.gov/parkhistory/online_books/hh/11/hh11b.htm.

"Timeline: The Statue of Liberty." *PBS*. 2002. http://www.pbs.org/kenburns/statueofliberty/timeline.

NANCY OHLIN is the author of the YA novels *Always, Forever* and *Beauty* as well as the early chapter book series Greetings from Somewhere under the pseudonym Harper Paris. She lives in Ithaca, New York, with her husband, their two kids, four cats, and assorted animals who happen to show up at their door. Visit her online at nancyohlin.com.

ROGER SIMÓ is an illustrator based in a town near Barcelona, where he lives with his wife, son, and daughter. He has become the person that he would have envied when he was a child: someone who makes a living by drawing and explaining fantastic stories.